T4-AHG-777

GOOD MORNING, LORD

Meditations for
Teachers

Donald Charles Mainprize

BAKER BOOK HOUSE
Grand Rapids, Michigan

**Dedicated
to
students
and
teachers
everywhere**

Copyright 1974 by
Baker Book House Company

ISBN: 0-8010-5959-3

First printing, November 1974
Second printing, April 1977
Third printing, June 1979

Printed in the United States of America

Premeeting Session

The poems and meditations offered here to teachers and administrators aim to renew an interest in quality learning and one-to-one relationships in our schools.

They should be received as thought-starters, not thought-stoppers. They call on us to make decisions, to urge action, or to provoke thinking that will increase learning in our own schools by our students.

These thoughts may appear too idealistic ever to be realized by the average teacher and school, but unless we aim high and hold our aim, we'll miss the target altogether. An aspiring quarterback does not study every move of Joe Smith, the kid down the street; he emulates Joe Namath or Fran Tarkenton.

If there are weaknesses in our schools, the good and the humane educators must move to the front lines. As Robert Louis Stevenson wrote: "You cannot run away from a weakness; you must some time fight it out or perish; and if that be so, why not now, and where you stand?"

Donald Charles Mainprize

Houghton Lake, Michigan
November 1974

1 The Break of the Day

Groggy
Grumpy
Owly
Ornery
Hungry

Good lord! Morning!

Focused
Cheerful
Chirpy
Sociable
Soulful

Good Morning, Lord!

*(Perhaps we might call this Breakfast
at Epiphanies.)*

An epiphany is a manifestation of the Lord. In the Christian year Epiphany is January 6, the day the wise men found Jesus. Wise teachers seek to breakfast with the Lord.

Someone has said that men should see the face of God before they see the face of men. If so, it's doubly true of teachers who daily face scores of students. Starting a day with thirty kids is traumatic enough, but to do so without having your spiritual eyes in focus is to invite trouble.

Students today need a teacher who is alert, friendly, and, even, inspiring. Kids come to us in all stages of emotional and spiritual disrepair. Some are near the breaking point, others at decisive crossroads. To act as a safety valve and to point out the best route takes a teacher with ears tuned in to the Holy Spirit and with eyes focused clearly enough to see beneath the facade of "playing it cool."

The teacher bogged down under his own personal burdens will find it onerous to take time to lift the burdens of others. The teacher who learns to leave his burden with the Lord in his quiet hour can be a blessing to kids.

O FATHER

Help me meet You at daybreak that I may share Your presence with my younger, less experienced brothers and sisters.

TODAY I WILL

Be of good cheer
because that's why I'm here.

BIBLE FRAGMENT: Luke 5:16.

2 It's All Greek

Perhaps   is   climb   wall
no   harder than   of
wall   to   a   words.

King Solomon wrote "... of making many books there is no end; and much study is a weariness of the flesh" (Eccles. 12:12). Some students, recognizing the truth of this statement, study as little as possible. Many, however, climb wearily over or through word after word. Some do it to learn for themselves, others to please their parents or teachers, and some to keep up with their friends.

For many, it's a weary, thankless, nerve-stretching struggle.

Perhaps no other single factor contributes so much frustration to a child than the inability to read the required book for the course. All too often the average teacher overlooks the obvious problem, or can see no way in her system to overcome the situation. With little effort one subconsciously labels the child as "slow," "disadvantaged," or "dumb." If the busy teacher neglects to consult previous tests in the permanent file or to give the child a diagnostic reading test, the educator is operating in the darkness of ignorance. Two visually handicapped people walking in the dark make learning a matter of chance.

School, with its unnatural routine of walk, sit,

don't talk, listen, write, read, answer, correct mistakes, *ad repetitio, ad nauseum, ad infinitum,* is bad enough for a child without his having to scale a barbed-wire wall of words every hour of the day to find out just what the book or the teacher wants.

What can you do to lighten the load for the student? What is your solution to his problem?

Think of yourself as a Good Samaritan having come upon a child beaten and bruised by bouncing off a fearsome phonic fence. The first step is the same as the Samaritan's: "He had compassion on him" (Luke 10:33). *Sans* compassion you might as well hang it up as a teacher, particularly, of the culturally deprived. See the child as your neighbor or younger brother. Pick up the victim where you found him—at his present reading level—and apply the proper learning prescription: books or tapes written at his level that meet his learning needs. Add daily doses of praise for any measure of success or effort.

O FATHER

Open my eyes to see the struggling, bleeding students in my classes who daily wrestle with words and lose too often.

TODAY I WILL

Choose one student, check his files, test him if necessary, and find some suitable materials he can read with success.

BIBLE FRAGMENT: Luke 10:25-37.

3 Festus Again

"Much learning doth make thee mad," is still the sad cry of too many a dad.

In A.D. 54, give or take a little, the governor of Caesarea voiced the philosophy of the parents of many of our children when he yelled to Paul of Tarsus, "Thou art beside thyself; much learning doth make thee mad" (Acts 26:24).

A friend of mine, a successful published author, has often told me of his father's ranting about the foolishness of "book-larnin." The attitude and actions of our students reflect their homes. If reading invites criticism at home, it will be considered useless in school. If at home a child is cut down for drawing pictures or writing, you can't expect him to get ecstatic in the classroom at the mention of art or creative writing.

The teacher unaware of this deep vein of anti-intellectualism expects his students to be automatically interested in a given subject, book, or lesson. That teacher needs to spend some time with parents.

A mother who never cracks a book, magazine, or newspaper in the presence of her kids may be a fine person, but she inadvertently makes the teacher's job twice as difficult. An industrious father who excels in manual labor probably has a son who needs vocational training, but since many schools do not provide it, he'll need an interest in reading and books to survive in the jungle of ink and paper.

The ink-stained, book-oriented pedagogue must think behind the face of the facts or she'll kill some of her students with ink-poisoning.

O FATHER

Teach me to individualize my teaching and meet the kids where they live with what they need, as You did for me.

TODAY I WILL

Find out why .... hates to read
And look beneath his skin to meet his need.

BIBLE FRAGMENT: Ecclesiastes 12:12 f.

4 "Having Eyes . . ."

I	at	I	the
taught	such	never	boy
first	a	did	without
semester	torrid	see	a
	pace		face.

The tragedy is that the visible kids get all the attention while the invisible ones are neglected. As the frontier proverb goes, "The squeakin' wheel gets the grease." Modern American public education is often a matter of greasing squeaky wheels in the form of slow students and discipline problems while neglecting the quiet, dependable, bright and not-so-bright students.

The unseen come in several shapes or sizes. Some are educationally handicapped but manage to overachieve anyway. Others have physical problems such as overweight, underweight, severe acne, scars, or homeliness, any of which make it easier for them to bury themselves in the books. Some are mentally slow, but determined to excel; while a few are bright, but shy.

Whatever their problem, many of these unseen suffer from neglect; innocent neglect, I mean. Perhaps the severest test of a teacher's judgment comes when he is served a time pie of 45 minutes and told to slice it into 35 pieces. Presuming he gives equal time to each student, he has 77 seconds for each. That amounts to 6 minutes and 25 seconds per week per student or 3 hours and 51 minutes per student per 180-day year. The wonder of American education is the fact that kids learn anything.

And one major reason they do learn is the presence of the invisible kids. But I think it demeans the invisibles some to be overlooked, to get second-class treatment when they have first-class minds.

By going out of our way to let them know we see them, we show we appreciate their worth, and we build a bridge over which they may wish to visit us.

Naturally we see our students daily, but to see is not to *see*. To discuss or show genuine interest in a special project, an independent study, a poem, or any aspect of a child's school or non-school life is to *see*. And it's this personal touch that opens doors to enjoyable learning, and it probably is the most important element in quality education. Let it not be said that, "Having eyes, you see not."

O FATHER

Get my eyes off all the problem kids long enough to see the steady, dependable kids that are America's greatest asset.

TODAY I WILL

Choose at least two kids per day to single out for praise this week. I will give them my full attention when I talk to them so they will know I care.

BIBLE FRAGMENT: Isaiah 6:9.

5 As a Rule

He
who
lectures
by
the
yard
usually
teaches
by
the
inch.

One of the greatest illusions of teachers is that their words carry great weight and insight and light and—therefore—they should talk . . . and talk . . . and talk.

The trouble is, many teachers do not have training in public speaking, and, at their best, they are boring.

The teacher who attempts to individualize knows that only some kids can learn by listening and even the most advanced can not withstand a thirty-minute barrage of verbiage every hour.

The essence of teaching, of course, is helping kids learn—and individual conversations aimed at dealing with the child's own learning weakness are of far greater value than lengthy lectures in which half of the kids get lost in the first five paragraphs and suffer added frustrations as the talker continues to wall himself in and the student out.

No one argues for the completely silent teacher. Short explanations or mini-lectures from five to ten minutes long are probably all the kids in grades one to eight can absorb anyway. So why not forget the long lecture cop-out and deal with the kids' needs directly in mini-lectures or individual conversations with plenty of chances for questions.

O FATHER

Help me to shut my mouth long enough that my ears can have a chance to hear and learn the real needs of kids.

TODAY I WILL

Spend more time preparing my explanations so that the words and illustrations I choose will shed light yet not get lost in a forest of verbal foliage.

BIBLE FRAGMENT: Proverbs 17:27.

6 The End of Love

When
you
quit
loving
all
students,
you've
quit
loving
the
Teacher.

For those of us who do not remember—it is a fearful thing to fall into the hands of an anxious pedagogue in a strange classroom. Especially when several unpleasant things happen in classrooms, such as having your ignorance exposed by a wrong answer to an easy question, being laughed at for stumbling over your own feet, being whispered about for wearing old, out-of-style hand-me-downs, being trimmed down for breaking a rule you really haven't heard about, or being slandered by a heartless teacher.

Probably half of the guff kids lay on us stems from fear, and is a defensive reaction which wouldn't be necessary if they didn't feel threatened.

Let us learn the art of scaling kids' defensive walls with the hands and feet of love. If we will touch the inner lives of the empty, the weary, and the lonely kids in our classrooms, we will have contributed immensely to the peace of the future and the future of peace.

And—though some would deny it—there's no better way to a kid's mind than through his heart.

O FATHER

Teach me the truth that perfect love casts out fear and let Your love shine in my classroom through me.

TODAY I WILL

Choose one or two students, either the unassuming sort, or the problem kind, and by a touch of love, a look of love, or by giving them some time, I'll let them know I care.

BIBLE FRAGMENT: Matthew 22:37, 38, **39.**

7 Uppers and Downers

Your
students
will
get
you
down,
if
you're
not
prayed
up.

Paul's words cover this truth. He wrote, "Happy is the man who condemneth not himself in that thing which he alloweth" (Rom. 14:22c).

If you're happy not condemning yourself for what you allow, then the opposite is also true: you'll be miserable if you must condemn yourself for what you let happen in your class.

If you're "up a tree," "climbing the walls," or nearly "out of your mind," it's because *you* allowed it. Don't blame Sara Jones, the principal, the school board, or the parents.

If an intolerable situation exists, change it by prayer and action. Don't allow it to infect other students, or yourself. Get help from colleagues, superiors, friends and stay with it until change comes.

It is not wrong if the devil sneaks his way into the rooms of your mind; it is wrong if you offer him a chair.

Every teacher will meet unruly youngsters sooner or later. You will either rule them by love and firmness and prayer, or they will rule you, and, if you let them, they'll become the Achilles heel of your teaching career.

O FATHER

Teach me to be fair, firm, friendly, and forgiving with those who would disrupt class, even as You have with me.

TODAY I WILL

Exercise friendly firmness with those who have difficulty controlling their actions and take positive steps to change any intolerable situations in my classroom.

BIBLE FRAGMENT: Ephesians 5:18-20.

8 An Assessment of Differential Evaluation

The	certain	is	does
only	about	that	it
thing	grading	everyone	differently.

No two grades, though both the same, mean the same thing in today's educational scene. Seldom do two teachers grade alike. One teacher uses letters A, B, C; another uses a numerical percentage 93, 80, 75; others use only Pass or Fail; some use no grades; and still others curve scores with the highest receiving A's and the lowest E's.

No matter which method one uses, certain factors must be kept in mind. A grade should involve a careful consideration of the student's capability, ability, and effort. You need to correlate three factors: what he has achieved, what he could have been expected to achieve, how much effort he put forth.

In all fairness, a student who could have done a great deal of work and learning and didn't, due to laziness, does not deserve as high a grade as a student who could have done only a little, but *did* that little with great *effort*.

Another important factor in grading is the nature of your teaching and the facet of your subject covered in a given term. Transformational grammar may come hard for some, easy for others; whereas writing descriptions may be a snap for A, but a bear for B.

Teaching methods make a difference also. Some kids do better on textbook work, others on audio-visuals, some dig lectures, and some fare better on a combination.

The better you know your student's mental, emotional, and social weakness, the fairer your grade will be, providing you consider these factors when you grade him.

Barring a major revolution of the grass roots variety, grades will be around for a decade or two yet. Since they mean so much to children and many parents, the least we can do is dispense them with every ounce of fairness at our command while we campaign either for their abolition or some consistency in grading, locally or nationally.

If God judged us as inconsistently and unfairly as many of us evaluate students, we'd rise up and demand His dismissal, in spite of His long-standing tenure.

O FATHER
Thank You for judging me with fairness, impartiality, consistency, and compassion.

TODAY I WILL
Inquire about others' methods of grading or locate and read an article on grading, or check journals for a conference on grading.

BIBLE FRAGMENT: John 7:24.

9 Quickie Assignments, Rotten Examinations, and Other Vices

If that students Egads!
you covers studied, What
design exactly everyone then?
a test what might
pass.

Someday, along with a book on students' responsibilities in learning, someone should write a book classifying teachers' vices. I speak of such vices as *assuming* all students possess inherent motivation for *my* subject, or expecting that even the dumb kids (I speak as a fool) should understand *my* vocabulary, *my* illustrations—in case I provide any, or believing that one explanation is enough if the kids would just shut up and listen, or giving out thirty-second, incomprehensible assignments five seconds before the bell rings, or after.

It's bad enough to be an unwilling member of a captive audience without being forced to do something you can't understand and being graded for how well you do it. Since students must weather the school scene one way or another, they ask mother or another student, or they muddle through and get the inevitable low grade.

This frustration could have been eliminated if the teacher had taken more time telling the unit's or subject's value to the kids, explaining in several ways the examples, problems, sentences, or whatever, or perhaps, letting a student rephrase the assignment, or mimeographing the assignment or a group of them, for each student.

As our poem indicates, a person needs to be readied—prepared—to be able to learn some things, and a student deserves a test that covers only the material presented, not some obscure section or chapter not even assigned. Teachers should remember that anyone can devise a test that will stump and flunk the brightest of philosophers.

Some teachers, and more than a few, are slaves to finishing so many pages or units by a certain date. To do so, they shove, drag, or push as many students as possible along the road of learning, scarring many in the process. Their slogan seems to be, "I have yet many things to say unto you—" and they keep on talking, forgetting that talking is not always teaching.

O FATHER
Help me to learn the art of preparing the minds of children for the giving of assignments that are clear, complete, and comprehensible.

TODAY I WILL
Find anything I can in print on the art of giving assignments and designing just and equitable evaluations.

BIBLE FRAGMENT: John 16:12.

10   Adult Reactor?

If   based
your   on
peace   how
of   teen-agers
mind   act,
in   you
class   are
is   hurtin'.

In spite of the youth of many teachers these days, a teacher should be a person of stability, able to cope with kids at their worst without going into shock, hurling curses or insults, or breaking down emotionally.

Some teachers, however, assume that it's the child's major responsibility to avoid upsetting them. Such is not the case, although students do have specific responsibilities. Yet as kids see it (many of them) their task is to survive six hours a day with six different jailers, and still eke out a bit of enjoyment. As an aside they have to please the jailer, mom and dad, the warden, and their inner selves, in the matter of grades and behavior.

Since the jailer sentences the students to mental labor, he can not expect to be sheltered and coddled by the prisoner, his victim. In fact, some degree of hostility can be expected from many kids not conditioned to the unnatural world of books, paper, writing, and exams.

Naturally each teacher establishes his own level of tolerance, in terms of the amount of noise, physical activity, talking, and work accomplished. That that limit is constantly challenged and sometimes passed by students is no surprise; but when a teacher allows it to be exceeded and then throws a verbal fit—he is to blame.

One must reassess his tolerance point occasionally and change it if necessary, bearing in mind that it's not student action or inaction that trees us—it's our *reactions*. Your tranquillity had better not depend solely on the actions of those around you.

O FATHER
Teach me to manage my life by Your Spirit's power and not to depend on others' co-operation for my peace of mind.

TODAY I WILL
Aim to be at my best emotionally and spiritually when kids are at their worst.

BIBLE FRAGMENT: Isaiah 26:3.

11 Past Graduate Studies or Post Graduate Studies?

I
never
met
a
good
teacher
who
wasn't
still
learning.

We've all been reminded of the retiring teacher who, it was said, taught one year, forty times. We laugh and bury our stack of annual plans and goals a bit deeper in our file lest someone discover its year-to-year similarity.

There's no harm, clearly, in staying with a winning game plan as long as you're undefeated. It's frightening, however, to be reminded that every year brings new rule changes in the game of learning. Or to discover that you ought to be a learning coordinator (catalyst), instead of an ever-verbalizing artesian well of knowledge. Or to hear, via the gripevine, that one day, perhaps soon, someone will be around to ask you if you know what you've been doing all year (accounta-bility), or measure how well you've done it (assessment).

By informal interviewing here and there I've learned that: many teachers do not belong to the national or state organization of their teaching area, that few subscribe to the journal of their discipline, and that fewer still read the current research in their field.

Where do you fit in this classification? Are you growing professionally? If you are not a growing teacher, chances are you're a routine, run-of-the-mill, obsolete pedagogue. He who would instill a love for learning in others, must love it himself.

Would your Lord consider you a dedicated professional?

O FATHER
Teach me the value of learning. Remind me, daily, that I ought to excel, "heartily, as to the Lord, and not unto men. . . ."

TODAY I WILL
Read a journal in my field or a book written to help me improve as a teacher. Or—con-sider joining the national organization of my field.

BIBLE FRAGMENT: Colossians 3:17, 23-24.

12 A Jekyll and Hyde Original

*Behind   parents
some   who
wild   couldn't
students   be
are   more
two   surprised.*

I'll not soon forget the day I met Tom Beebee's parents. Since then, I've always wondered why teachers neglect contacting parents as an early step in handling classroom disturbances.

Tom was lazy, doing as little as possible of any assignment, and that little only when I hovered over him like a police helicopter, forgetting my thirty-three other students.

His work was sloppy, his papers and pencil were "in my locker," and worse yet, he kept his papers in the popular 2 1/2" x 2 1/2" denim pocket filing system which frequently passed through the Kenmore on weekends.

Naturally, I nagged, handed out noon hours, deducted points for sloppiness, and, in general, made life in my class unpleasant for both of us.

Then one night at a library function I met Tom's parents. Mr. Alfred Beebee was a successful, self-motivated salesman, representing his company in half of the state. He was a serious, well-organized person. Al was concerned about his son's education and glad to discuss Tom's school life.

Evelyn, his wife, seemed no less concerned. Both were surprised that Tom's midterm progress report was negative, and that his responsibility for classwork had nosedived from his previous school. For reasons of his own, Tom had decided to excel in laziness, to do as little as possible.

The next Monday Tom had a sectioned notebook, a supply of pencils, and, most important, a new attitude. Now and then he backslides, but the loving firmness at home has released one police helicopter from making frequent buzzes over Row 1, seat 3.

O FATHER
Remind me that many parents want to know how their kids act at school and want to take part in their education.

TODAY I WILL
Watch for those Jekyll and Hyde kids and use the phone to enlist parents' back-up in the all important job of building men and women for tomorrow's world.

BIBLE FRAGMENT: Proverbs 29:17.

13 About the Size of It

No   some
matter   parents
what   are
their   very
size   small.

Parents come in all shapes and sizes, but it's their interior mindscape that their kids emulate and it's their self-centered life style that the kids hate because it shuts kids out and turns kids off.

Some of these children were born because their parents enjoyed sex—not because they wanted children. Offspring were, so to speak, a necessary evil. Such children are tolerated, used, and mistreated. The major advantage of school is that it babysits the kids almost eight hours a day. Other places that help these parents enjoy their lives are the street—where their kids spend a lot of time, the kids' friends, where parents encourage their kids to visit often, and school activities at night, which give parents another night out, or in front of the TV, with no kids to harass them with long hair, sassy mouths, and insane moods.

These parents pay loud lip service to teachers and education while with the teachers at school because John got kicked out of class or school, or failed his subjects. They say, "You tell me what he's supposed to do, and I'll see he does it." But don't expect them to attend John's sports activities or to take more than a report-card interest in his studies.

They have more important things to do, such as bowl twice a week, go to card parties, or Stanley parties, or the local pub.

As one boy put it, "My parents use me. I'm their errand boy. The car sits home all day while mother watches TV serials and makes a list of errands for me to run as soon as I hit the door."

A girl adds, "It wouldn't be so bad if my mother wasn't so lazy. We have to do the day's dishes, iron our own clothes, and clean the house. What does she do all day?"

By their actions such parents say loud and clear: "Learning is not important. Living is. Self-satisfaction is the name of the game, not sacrifice for the sake of kids. I come first, the kids get what is left."

And we wonder why kids cause trouble in class. We may be the only safety valve some of our kids have.

O FATHER

Help me to learn that educating parents is also a part of helping kids learn.

TODAY I WILL

Take steps to encourage parents to find out what goes on in my room by visiting my classes, and, I will read what other teachers are doing to build positive home-school relations.

BIBLE FRAGMENT: Proverbs 2:6-11.

14   Minus Ninety and Holding

I

Let me see now
Was it Xerxes or Xenophon
(Both names I *must* remember)
Who killed the joy of learning
On that warm day in November?

A soft wind in your face, a walk in a technicolor forest, talking with your best friend, a swim in a balmy lake with your girl, working on your car, playing touch football on your corner lot, these are the natural actions of a free life.

A stack of books, assignments, pencils, silence, Pavlovian reactions to bells, walking, controlled thinking, sitting, answering, listening, these are the unnatural actions of an enslaved life.

So goes the propaganda from Kidsville.

And, as usual, some truth dwells in both abodes. But with the genius of American synthesis some schools have married Outdoor Education to the Open Classroom and their child represents the best of both worlds.

Some danger lies in two areas: the possibility of learning next to nothing of subject content while running about hither and yon exercising freedom and the art of inquiry, and the pandering of weakened, amused TV-oriented mentalities by innovations designed to entertain lazy minds.

The fact, somewhere supported, that men use

only 10 percent of their mental capacity leads me to wonder what we could do if we were badgered into stretching our capacity.

I recall vividly, as a child, not only my general disenchantment with teachers and students, but also my insatiable quest for, and satisfaction with, what I found in books, and my joy at learning things at school or at home that I had never known before. Learning was fun, and still is.

Perhaps it's neither Xerxes, nor T-rel transformations that killed the joy of learning. It may just be a natural affliction common to young and old alike:

II

Perhaps by thinking my way back
Through trials and fears and haziness
I'd find the real trouble was
With my confounded laziness.

O FATHER

Assist me in bridging the gap between kids' world and the world of schools, and to apportion a fair share of the responsibility for learning between myself and them.

TODAY I WILL

Discuss with my favorite teacher exactly how much work she requires from students daily or weekly.

BIBLE FRAGMENT: Proverbs 2:1-6.

15 "A Little Child . . ."

Some	*would*
parents	*only*
would	*follow*
learn	*the*
a	*footsteps*
lot	*of*
if	*their*
they	*kids.*

I remember calling in the home of a student who had been ill a lot. She was as neat a child with her books and assignments and desk as you could imagine, but her home was a low-class pig pen. There were puddles on the floor where her younger brothers and sisters had tracked in with wet and muddy footgear. On the table were unwashed dishes from at least two days' meals. Her parents could learn from her.

One boy in school won a contest on cleaning up the environment but his parents had never learned the lesson. Their residence was a neighborhood eyesore and had been so all during their ten-year occupancy.

Tom was the quietest boy in school and you'd think his parents would be top-class. They both came in one day for consultation about Tom's sister. The mother was a loudmouthed foreman type whose behavior embarrassed Tom so much he missed two days of school after his parents' visit.

One of the best, but most neglected, methods of getting to know kids and why they act as they do at school is to meet their parents in their home. It will surely prove one of my epigrams, "The trouble with some kids is apparent."

O FATHER

Help me to represent a good father to those who've never seen one, so they will come to respect You as Father.

TODAY I WILL

Praise at least three students for their cheerfulness and cooperation.

BIBLE FRAGMENT: Job 32:5-9.

16 The Lasting Legacy

The
only
lasting
thing
we
have
to
give
students
is
love.

To understand the might of love we need to see that the result of love is friendship, and that friendship demands expression in words and actions.

How can I so talk and act that no one will question my concern or the fact that I wish to be a friend? Let's consider speech. I must not frequently dress a child down publicly, call him names, or say things to him privately that he can interpret as reflecting dislike. Neither should I make a great verbal fuss over other students at the expense of, and in the presence of, this child. One's mouth can hurt sensitive, immature kids.

Actions also tell tales that young kids interpret for themselves. A special *look* at Kim, and another girl feels slighted or wonders if that look helps Kim's grade. An icy stare at a poor child, a homely child, or a crippled child will turn off many kids and they'll spot you as a phony.

Naturally—all kids will never like every teacher. They may do well to tolerate some, but make sure the bridge from you to them reaches all the way over all rivers. They must step out—but with every assurance the bridge won't give way.

Only God the Spirit can shed love to every boy and girl and help you to be a channel of love.

O FATHER
Fill me with love for the Spirit
and the Spirit of love.

TODAY I WILL
Check my thoughts, actions, attitudes, and words to see if my love is spread out impartially.

BIBLE FRAGMENT: Romans 5:5.

17 Empathy Training

Two of the worst problems a teacher can have are to forget what it was like to be a kid; and the other one is to review one's life every day in class.

"I don't think old Stoneface was ever a teenager," goes the hall talk. "She won't even let us hold hands." This quote highlights *our* preoccupation with the present and *our* forgetfulness about our early teen years.

If one of the main developmental tasks of early teen life is growth in social awareness (Havighurst and Taba), then we would do well to recognize this and bend a little when kids get moody because of a boy-girl problem, linger in the hall until beyond the last minute (*their* job is growing up, school is a secondary problem), or get too close together in the halls.

A deep, thorough meditation on our teen years and school life once a week would give us a better vantage point from which to understand our students.

Almost as bad as forgetting is remembering.

"I learned almost nothing about algebra, but I could easily write Mr. Smith's *Memoirs*. That class is a snap, just get him talking about his days with the taxicab company. He'll go on for hours."

Sometimes a bit of reminiscence, strategically given, strengthens one's teaching. If overdone, it's boring, laughable, and indefensible.

O FATHER

Remind me of my youth and help me empathize.

TODAY I WILL

Meditate for ten minutes on my school years, the problems and the joys, and relate my reactions to the problems specific kids have at school today.

BIBLE FRAGMENT: I Timothy 4:15.

18   The Fairness Doctrine

I	was
would	fair
rather	than
have	an
a	excellent
fair	teacher
teacher	who
who	wasn't.

One of the most common plaints of kids is that teachers aren't fair. And too often, they're correct. And, in many cases, kids are powerless to strike back, directly or indirectly.

Some parents—more than a few—still look upon teachers as semigods who almost never are wrong. *Ergo*—regardless of junior's attempts to explain, he's bound to lose. Many principals, too, tend to line up with the teacher—even before a complete hearing is held.

It's highly possible that Mr. Teacher could have blown it, lost his temper, or acted unfairly. At any rate an impartial hearing would start with that assumption also.

Just what is fairness? Is it fair to allow thirty seconds at the end of class to give a complicated assignment and then to hand out E's if it's not completed or if the work is done incorrectly? Is it fair to explain a problem once, refuse to explain it again, then give E's for incorrect work?

Is it *just* to become visibly angry when a student says he doesn't understand a third or fourth time? What sort of justice is it to assign six specific chapters for a test and then give a test that covers an extra chapter or two? What is just about setting a deadline for a class to have work in, have several students sacrifice substantially to get the work in, then have the teacher reschedule the test or deadline for those who goofed off?

What's fair about embarrassing a student in front of the class, or calling him stupid? (If you think this isn't done, start listening to kids, or to teachers in the lounge.)

O FATHER
Help me to be impartial with students while recognizing their individual differences and abilities.

TODAY I WILL
Act kindly toward those I tend to naturally dislike.

BIBLE FRAGMENT: Romans 2:11.

19 "Thanks, Will"

All
that
fritters
is
not
goaled.

With all the debate on Performance Objectives in books, magazines, conventions, and on faculties, one might think there was some question about the value of knowing what we're doing and of doing our job in an organized, efficient manner.

I should think we have operated long enough on the will and whim of each teacher who, in many cases, has been a law unto himself. If we wish to maintain some quality control in the educational process, we'll have to know what constitutes "quality" in content, in achievement, and in effort.

We will not succeed unless we start working individually and collectively with learning objectives in the light of individual differences, and unless we hammer out some generally accepted standards of adequate performance for promotion.

Bible readers are encouraged to "go on," to "do all things heartily," and to "do all things decently and in order." Yet I've noticed that only about three or four out of ten teachers subscribe to their own professional journal, let alone keep up on relevant research.

The current stress on assessment, accountability, and performance objectives will take a decade or two to reach the hinterlands. Although individual Christian teachers will assess these factors differently, we can not indifferently reject the principles of measuring our accomplishments, of giving an account of the use of our ability, and of stressing that specific objectives be achieved by our students.

Jesus Himself referred to all of the domains of learning when He said, "If ye know these things (cognitive), happy are ye (affective), if ye do them (psychomotor)" John 13:17.

O FATHER

Help me to avoid wasting my time, my preparation period, and my energy, by not knowing my teaching goals and how to achieve them.

TODAY I WILL

Exercise myself in knowing what's new in my field, attending at least one conference, and subscribing to the journal of my field.

BIBLE FRAGMENT: I Thessalonians 5:21.

20 On Esoteric Jargon

Except as a enter
ye small the
be child, door
converted ye of
and shall the
speak not mind.

A friend of mine, a successful teacher, tells me she never lectures anymore because, "It's probably the worst method of communicating."

I tend to avoid long lectures in favor of mini-lectures, five to ten minutes long, and then only when absolutely necessary. I recall a lecturer at seminary whose every word was not only poly-syllabic, but incomprehensible. Most of us college graduates were still decoding our notes on Thursday of a five-day lecture series.

My point is that a truly educated teacher must find where his learners live in terms of listening vocabulary and stay somewhere within that range while at the same time he gradually adds to students' knowledge and word bank.

The too-typical pedant appears tempted to think that snowing listeners under a barrage of high-sounding verbosity has some real relation to teaching. One comes away having watched and listened to an ego-trip "Filled with sound and fury—signifying nothing."

Perhaps Paul's words to the Corinthians would be good advice to teachers: "And I, brethren, when I came to you, came not with excellency of speech or of wisdom, declaring unto you the testimony of God. . . . And my speech and my preaching was not with enticing words of man's wisdom . . ." (I Cor. 2:1, 4a).

In reading of the reactionaries' attack on new math in California, one wonders if perhaps the new math and new English publishers should recycle their textbooks through the strainer of common sense and shave the vocabulary level and syllable count down to the level of a fifth-grader. Then we teachers and parents could understand them also.

O FATHER

I thank You for the simplicity of the gospel message of forgiveness.

TODAY I WILL

Screen by conscious choice my messages to kids to avoid pedantry and, more important, to get behind the closed doors of their minds.

BIBLE FRAGMENT: I Corinthians 8:1.

21 Youth and Me

*Youth
recognizes
youth,
regardless
of
age.*

Paul wrote that the Corinthians had to be spoken to as "babes." Perhaps no other truth, if taken to heart, would be so effective in helping us see and assess ourselves and our students in the light of true wisdom and honest humility.

If each of us could take an effective SQ test and discover our spiritual age, we might hastily re-apply for admission in the school of God— elementary section.

How easy it is for our age and physical size and position to lead us to think of ourselves as superior and wiser in all things than those younger and smaller and with less seniority. As Elihu, we believe that "Days should speak, and multitude of years should teach wisdom." But— also as Elihu, we should remember that "Great men are not always wise; neither do the aged understand judgment" (Job 32:7, 9).

Assuredly, competent teachers will seek to remain healthy by periodic self-examinations, and will take the proper treatment. The ailing ones should be encouraged to drop out or seek help and take their medicine as mature learners.

Let us speak candidly about the *necessity* of understanding, compassion, in-service training, behavioral objectives, *adequate lesson planning*, acceptable speech and behavior in the classroom and the students' rights not to be slandered for failure—due either to laziness or lack of ability.

O FATHER

Help us, as teachers, to learn that self-judgment is a necessary continual process if teaching is to be respected as a profession.

TODAY I WILL

Encourage other teachers to excel by commenting on helpful articles I have read or by raising the issue of quality teaching in a discussion.

BIBLE FRAGMENT: Proverbs 28:13.

22 Teacher vs. Textbook

Even	a	you
if	textbook	in
you	can	front
can't	not	of
read	yell	the
it,	at	class.

Although it would be comfortable to say it doesn't happen, it does; and it's no fun to be yelled at, insulted, or otherwise embarrassed in front of a class of thirty or thirty-five fellow students.

One of the easiest things to forget as a teacher is how fearful and long is the path up to the teacher's desk. Many are the snares that keep a child from seeking help, even though he needs and wants it desperately.

Will he yell at me? Call me stupid, like one teacher did? Will he use my wrong answer as an example of what not to do? Will she notice my dirty fingernails? My wrinkled shirt? My dirty blouse? Does my breath smell?

High school teachers might think that such fears have passed, but they haven't; they've changed to hostility or bitterness.

By varying his tone of voice, a teacher can say, "You dummy," or "I'm so much more intelligent than you," or "I have little respect for you." Harshness, sarcasm, epithets, and frowns all send out messages of dislike and disgust, and, in so doing, impede learning. Whatever their value as discipline tools, they should be used sparingly and with deliberation.

O FATHER
Help me to learn to create a wholesome learning climate that combines friendliness and factual firmness without name-calling or nagging.

TODAY I WILL
Watch for the fearful ones and allay their tenseness with the calming power of friendship.

BIBLE FRAGMENT: Proverbs 18:24, *RSV*.

23   The Call

He
who
is
not
dedicated
is
not
educated.

It may seem old-fashioned to speak of being called to teach—as if one needs a Damascus experience to teach math, social studies, or whatever.

Certainly such remarkably clear leading makes one fully aware that teaching is God's will for him. But "calls" come in all shapes and sizes, from a loud, booming voice to a quiet, calm whisper, or even a growing assurance that one is doing the will of God.

The key to one's vocation—whatever it is—is that it be the will of God for him. Then one can fulfill his calling by performing his role wholeheartedly, ". . . as unto the Lord, and not unto men" (Col. 3:23).

The person called of God to teach should be an example of the best in his teaching field, for as Solomon wrote, "Whatsoever thy hand findeth to do, do it with thy might" (Eccles. 9:10).

Do you work for the principal or The Principal? Are you called a teacher or called to teach?

O FATHER

Remind me that You are my employer and that I am called to train the minds of children made in Your image.

TODAY I WILL

Examine my workday to see if my attitudes and actions are worthy of Your name.

BIBLE FRAGMENT: Ephesians 5:17.

24 Mental Malnutrition

One	that	diet
trouble	*few*	*providing*
with	*administrators*	*even*
schools	*have*	*minimum*
today	*established*	*annual*
is	*a*	*requirements.*

(And fewer yet insist their requirements be met by everyone.)

Professional nutritionists have placed high value on knowing what good nutrition is and on establishing specific standards to be met to insure proper growth and vitality for infants, children, youth, and adults. Yet "man shall not live by bread alone."

What is proper growth and vitality for the mind? What are the minimums necessary to insure adequate grade-to-grade growth? Who has, or is, taking the time to see that Johnny's mind is growing adequately and healthily?

We who know the Master teacher must lead in preserving at least some minimal educational standards if we hope to live in a country where an educated citizenry tries to govern itself. If requirements tailspin or their realization lags, we will find ourselves schooling more and more students but they will be learning less and less.

This is, in fact, the case in many schools. Students graduate unable to read, spell, write, or figure adequately. This is the result of social promotion or the tendency to move students on—not knowing exactly how much they should know anyway, nor how to handle them should they fail to meet minimal requirements a year or so in a row.

O FATHER

Our minds are made in Your image. Help us to train adequately those minds in our care in the basic skills needed for successful living.

TODAY I WILL

Research the question of promoting ignorance by a lack of quality control at each grade level, and seek for reasonable workable remedies.

BIBLE FRAGMENT: Hebrews 5:12.

25   High Rise Deportment

Many	says
a	for
teacher	the
loses	third
his	time,
cool	"I just
when	don't
a	get
student	it."

Probably every teacher has felt the irritation in this poem. It's so easy to assume that the student must be a complete dunce not to understand *my* explanation. Or easier yet, to presume the student is putting you on to keep from getting at his work.

In either case, anger is no answer.

The answer may lie in examining the student's CA39's. You may have left the student months ago in terms of comprehension. Or you may be forcing a mental baby to climb an intellectual's mountain.

Another answer may be in your overreactions to kids' questions. If a teacher is unapproachable, a student will get answers from others, rather than face the teacher.

At first they'll tell Mom or Dad or other kids, but not you. Later, they tell you and you don't hear or believe—or you show anger.

It is embarrassing enough the first time to have to say, "I don't get this." It is humiliating to repeat it, but downright infuriating when the one paid to help you, becomes angry when you ask for help.

O FATHER
Help me to hear the timid, see the struggling, and bind up those I've already wounded.

TODAY I WILL
Listen for the cries of the confused and needy. I'll choose one whom I know is struggling and help him along the way.

BIBLE FRAGMENT: Luke 24:25-26.

26 The Heart of Understanding

Want
to
understand
others?
Take
a
long,
honest
look
at
yourself
and
you
will
be
humbled.

Are you ever late for appointments? Do you fail to get reports in on time? Have you ever talked to a person seated beside you when a teacher or administrator was "teaching"? Have you ever mislaid or forgotten to bring necessary papers to a class or meeting? Have you ever felt rotten or like doing nothing? Or like daydreaming?

If you answered affirmatively, bear this in mind the next time a student "blows" it, and treat him accordingly.

I make no excuses for the immature behavior of youngsters; I only hope we'll recognize and admit to the same immaturity in ourselves. Nothing comes easier than maintaining a solid aura of superiority when dealing with those younger and less disciplined than ourselves. Naturally the timid, the self-conscious, and the proper kids will not rebuke us. It takes either a brash, keen-witted child or a person with whom one vibes to make one see himself.

If such kids act as mirrors in which we see our warped reflection, it will be to no avail if we never get close enough to the mirror to get the picture.

Some teachers consider it professional to maintain a cool, detached, "paper" relationship with their students. This may just be a buffer zone, a smoke screen, or a wall to shut ourselves in and our students out. To each his own. But—unless you want to be the kind of self-centered, egotistical, tyrannical type teacher whose name is Legion, remember that the art of understanding is the understanding heart.

O FATHER
Help me to examine and to evaluate my inner being and outer habits and see how far I fall short of my expectations for others.

TODAY I WILL
Attempt, at least, during one class hour, to watch my words, actions, and thoughts for unwarranted symptoms of supposed superiority.

BIBLE FRAGMENT: Galatians 6:1-2.

27 On Life and Love

He
who
has
stopped
loving
is
dead
while
he
liveth.

A major problem in teaching is that both kids and teachers are human and immature. Just as kids say, "Ugh, I have Miss Panelli for English," teachers say, "I got another Manley kid this year, in my first hour yet."

We expect kids, however, to show their feelings and react negatively to those they dislike, but for teachers to do so is clearly a form of immaturity. It is also a sort of not-so-silent discrimination.

Naturally a certain number of kids will not like us, just as *we* do not all have the same set of friends. In spite of their obvious dislike of us, however, our reaction should be one of sincere acceptance of them—bad actions, attitudes, and all. They are, after all, just kids trying to grow up—a rather fearful task actually. So we try to love all students impartially, leaning over backwards to not show favoritism to the bright, the likable, the popular, or the nice-looking.

If anything, the slow, the unpopular, the shy, and the homely need our attention more than the successful. And, in terms of results, our efforts with the outsiders may be more rewarding and fruitful than with the insiders.

O FATHER

Let me see through the *persona,* the mask, and recognize Your likeness and image in all those to whom You've called me to teach. If I see Your likeness, how shall I not love them?

TODAY I WILL

Observe my normal actions and reactions to both the outsiders and insiders and examine them carefully for favoritism.

BIBLE FRAGMENT: Romans 12:9a.

28 Precocious Reminiscence

I
remember
when
I
used
to
enjoy
learning,
then
I
went
to
school.

On the basis of my intuitive research, only about four out of every ten kids in an average school find much enjoyment in the process of gaining an education. For the rest it's a bore and a chore.

A chore for some because they can't read the textbook for the class. Experts tell us that students in any one class may vary in reading ability by at least three grade levels. So—an eighth grade text may be given to a child with a fifth-grade reading level and the fight is on.

If this child is in the 60 percent who find little satisfaction in school, the word battle only frustrates him further. When you can't read, the whole school scene (almost) is a drag. Teacher after teacher piles pages on pages and words on words until you almost choke on paper. Grades sputter, parents sputter, and teachers sputter. In many schools no help is offered and there is no way to escape.

Perhaps a course should be devised on making physical incarceration interesting and maybe even fun. A step in this direction is individualized learning and prescription teaching. Another step would be to spend more time answering kids' questions about, and explaining the value of, the things we're asking them to learn. If we add to this picture, *less stress* on the time available to learn something, we would reduce the unnatural pressure. Actually, if something must be learned, the process of learning it need not be confined to a six-week course. What if the learning readiness and rate for that subject for some kids in the class is seven or even eight weeks? Shall we suspend the learning of that segment of knowledge and flunk those students who have not learned it at exactly 3:30 on Friday, February 8?

O FATHER
Help me to know what I should teach
to whom and when and why and how.

TODAY I WILL
Find or order a copy of *Educational Malpractices** by Don Stewart and read it to improve my teaching.

BIBLE FRAGMENT: John 16:12.

---

*SLATE Services, P.O. Box 456, Westminster, CA. 92683. $5.50.

29   On Building Railroads

*If
your
class
drives
you
up
the
wall,*

*it's
only
because
you
laid
the
tracks.*

Although most of the statistics in this book (or anywhere else for that matter) suffer from misinterpretation, distortion, exceptions, and inaccuracies, I'd judge that 80-90 percent of all discipline problems arise from the nature of the classroom atmosphere and the attitudes of the teacher—not from the student. And unless the classroom sensitivity is keyed—tuned up or down —controlled by the teacher, the students will "do that which is right in their own eyes."

One myth about open classrooms is that no one controls the throttle. The fact is that in a properly run open classroom both the fuel-injection system and the governors are most carefully adjusted. Indeed, more vigorous—though less obvious—controls are needed, else the room will jump the tracks.

The teacher who, through lack of planning, has no long-range or daily goals for himself or his students must expect trouble. Bad teachers cause more discipline problems than the students. The hard rule in a real school is organize or agonize.

To handle your charges with some measure of success in either open or traditional rooms you must have a clear aim for the day, either for some or all students, or individual aims for each. You ought to know where you're going and how you expect to get there.

If you're in the dark, don't expect your students to light the way. It's *your* bag. And even if you, like most of us, never had a class in exactly how to plan and organize, and teach, the bag is still stamped—Do-It-Yourself.

O FATHER
Burn into my mind that You are not the "author of confusion, but of peace," and help me get it all together in my room-world.

TODAY I WILL
Choose a teacher whom I respect and find out how he or she manages his room, check the journals for an article on planning, and set up an attainable, clear goal for one of my sections.

BIBLE FRAGMENT: Proverbs 25:28.

30 On the Value of Self-judgment

Having	I	lines	and
nothing	decided	judging	perhaps
better	to	my	a
to	write	own	few
do,	some	teaching	others'.

Many citizens today have set themselves up as fruit inspectors in the orchards of public education. Since the school has long been considered a strong third member of the Grand Tri-ad committed to developing American youth into a strong citizenry, such criticism is only natural. After all, one can not attack God and the Church too vigorously, and many parents, viewing the remains of their own shattered homes, criticize American homes and family life with as much vigor as a teen-ager making his bed.

Any organization, of course, which serves the public should expect criticism. And just as the best treatment for many a potential disease is prevention, so the best preparation for handling critics is self-criticism: policing one's profession, facing one's failings, extracting one's incurable organs.

It seems reasonable that those within a profession—given sufficient candor and acumen—should provide better treatment for their own ills than outsiders.

I know a thirteen-year-old boy who worked harder and showed more patience, proportionately, with one assignment than I had in preparing ten lesson plans.

I remember a thirteen-year-old girl who taught me more than twenty hours of education courses when she asked—seriously—one day, "Why can't learning be fun?"

As there are wide spans of grade levels in our classrooms, so are there vast differences in the social, mental, spiritual, and emotional maturity of teachers. A few minutes of observation in the lounge will reveal that.

The trick is not to know this truth: the trick is to let this truth set you free. Free to accept fellow teachers, students, and yourself, as immature, growing, changing, and learning children in the College of Love and Life. Once you experience and practice this truth, kids in your class will recognize your "youth" regardless of your age.

O FATHER

Forgive me for assuming spiritual superiority. Re-enroll me as a learner, and may Silence and Meditation be my first teachers.

TODAY I WILL

Let my classes write several paragraphs starting with the sentence, "If I were a teacher. . . ." These paragraphs I will read as prayerfully as if they were written by Dr. So and So from my State University.

BIBLE FRAGMENT: Galatians 6:3.